PHYSICO-PSYCHICO THERAPY

A Possible Breakthrough into Individual Healthiness and Sound Mindedness

Richard Oyovwevotu Efemuaye

For the Peace Merchants

PHYSICO - PSYCHICO THERAPY

A possible breakthrough into Individual Healthiness and SOUND MINDEDNESS

BY RICHARD OYOVWEVOTU EFEMUAYE

ISBN 978-978-923-205-5

Printed and Published by Creative Legacy Ventures,16B Aina Eleko Street Onigbongbo, Maryland, Lagos

DEDICATION

This book is dedicated to all MUSKITES all over the world. Also to members of Adejumo Lawn Tennis Club.

FOREWORD

The seeds of our heart today shall become the fruits of our lives tomorrow.

- The PMs

It has been well said that we should read a thing once, to find out what it contains; a second time, to understand it, a third time, to imprint it on our memory; a fourth time, we should repeat it silently to test ourselves whether we have firmly mastered it.

- John Comenius in "The Visible World"

PROLOGUE

If you can spare yourself some time and take a serious look at your body, you will notice at the slightest glance that this perfectly designed machine called the body is the vehicle assembled together by a perfect hand to transport you around the earth, explore the beauties of nature and experience life in abundance.

Like a prisoner in a prison room, you are imprisoned in a machine called the body having so many parts. If a man works hard enough to acquire a car, he drives it around until a time when it starts giving him discomfort (financial and psychological). He takes a decision on whether to abandon the car, forget about cars or buy another one. The driver of the car does not die with the car. It is the car that rots and rusts away when the driver has left it. Essentially, the car must be maintained, given proportionate energy, grease, engine oil and good petrol so that it will always be in good condition to take us to wherever we want to go.

Our body is a super machine, which is much more complex than the most complex artificial machine. Every part of it works in unison to enable us acquire as much experience as possible.

Apart from good food, which replaces the cells when they are aged and provides the body with potential energy for routine activities, there is a fundamental mechanism, which keeps the cells, the tissues, the organs etc. of the body constantly illuminated and activated.

This energy spreads from the heart to all other parts of the body. It is in the form of an internal light that illuminates the inside of the being just as the sun illuminates the external universe. This internal universe controlled by the light of the soul is linked with every part of the body from the systems to the organs to the tissues and to the cells. This is strongly linked with the light of procreation and that of the mind. The former is physically represented in the body by the sexual organs.

The light of the mind is represented physically by the brain. This is the way the energy that controls a human activity is distributed all over the body even to the fundamental building blocks of the body i.e. the cells. So if you look inside, it is like looking at the external universe with the sun as the center surrounded by light radiating planets.

This same energy is also carried by the blood cells along the blood stream. So, the inside of the human being is filled up with so much activity. This energy also controls the current on which the operations of the nerves are based.

Once there is a dwindle in the energy of any part of the body, that part starts a complicated process of decay which manifests externally as pain or ailment or infection.

This energy is in the form of a subtle light that can be amplified by the applicant to be as bright as any other source of light. This is a constant illumination from the heart to other parts of the body with the major centres in the brain, sexual parts, the eyes, the ears, the nostrils and on the tongue, the lungs, liver, the spleen, kidneys etc. These are like planets around the sun. This is the structure of the universe within. When this is known by an individual, he or she will not be paying all his attention to the external body but will become aware that there is something called a heartbeat, circulating blood to all parts of his body. This will lead you into looking and seeing internally. "Man know thyself".

If this energy system withdraws from all parts of the body into the heart and finally leaves, the heart stops beating. The body becomes numb (dead) and eventually begins the decay process, We do not want you to suffer foolishly as a result of the ignorance of the basic laws that govern the proper functioning of the LOVE between the light of the soul of man and the body, hence we have to explain some of the basic principles of Physico - Psychico Therapy to everyone, especially those who do not have the where-with-all to take medical trips abroad or foot the high hospital bills and those who do not like long needles and syringes around them. Do not forget that there is a school of thought, which is carrying out a campaign against the over medication of the world and her living things.

So if health is going to be for all in the NEAREST FUTURE, it could only be for people of an environment who have perfected the art of using their minds to direct light and consequently good health into even the tiniest cell of their ailing bodies. This is PPT- a possible and necessary supplement to orthodox and tradomedical practices.

Physico-Psychico Therapy involves the active and conscious use of the light within to effect activation and consequent cures on sick organs and tissues and cells. This is done through creative imagination, which is explained in the main body of this compilation.

Physico-Psychico Therapy also involves an exposition of the immense benefits one can acquire from active exercises of the body. Needless to say that physical exercise makes our physical body to be agile ready to explore the universe as human beings.

This book can also make a dull student to become clever and the clever one, more articulate due to the reorientation of the mind towards a more purposeful and creative thinking.

The compilation also talks about how PPT can be used to make the mind become an impregnable rock free from psychical attacks. The major change and transformation when you practise PPT is from self-consciousness to peace consciousness.

Please see the doctor if you cannot perfect and make PHYSICO-PSYCHICO THERAPY work for you.

The P.Ms

CHAPTER ONE

PEACE CONSCIOUSNESS

The mind of man is constantly bombarded by different impressions. These arise from environmental needs. We should not forget that the mind is the first expression of the soul, which he uses as the storehouse of past experiences, recorder of all present ones and a projector into the nature of future expressions. This means that the mind is the link between the REAL Self and the body. This REAL Self always yearns for experiences (good or bad). It is as a result of this that the REAL Self and the mind acquire a body that befits the kind of experiences required for a proper and positive expression on the evolutionary ladder. The mind of man must evolve. Nothing can stop it from acquiring the necessary experiences for him to climb higher and becoming more and more stable in the art of living. The mind gets its exercises by thinking and imagining possibilities and impossibilities. Many men have used their minds to turn the world around and you can do the same. Can you see power in the mind?

Much had been said, taught and written about the use of the mind. There are obviously hundreds of books, films and treatises which tell us how to get rich or how to get well or how to win friends by using the mind. These are all quite true. The mind is the most powerful instrument owned by man to move himself and creation around. But it is not easy for an average person like you and me to use the mind most effectively without first learning something about ourselves. If you would be a healer and bring healing strength to yourself and others, start it now -which you are already doing by reading this book. Everybody has the capacity to heal. It is known that the average human being uses just about 5% of his mind capability.

This same mind can be disturbed, like a bowl of water with ripples. To pick a coin from such a bowl accurately, is very difficult unless you are patient enough to allow the water in the bowl to calm down and the waves settle down.

The mind if disturbed by problems and worries is analogous to this bowl of disturbed water. If you want to consciously tap from all the experiences of the past imprinted in the dictionary of the mind, you have to clear it (the mind) of worries.

This can simply be done by gradually cultivating the belief that there is a ready receptacle for them and then, consciously lifting them (worries) into HIS MIGHTY HANDS.

To do this most successfully you have to become PEACE CONSCIOUS.

So, how do I become peace conscious and eventually have Peace of mind, in this world and life time? Teachers of old and new have always at one time or the other, been talking and teaching people about PEACE OF MIND.

If you want to start on the highway towards it, at least on earth, you must first be gradually attuned and conscious of your environment. I am also aware that this my body has a MIND. My mind is the bridge between my body and the energy keeping it alive. When this mind is not conditioned to harbour positive impulses of life, then, it gets out of rest and stops vibrating in unison with its immediate environment (the body). It becomes filled with worries and anxieties.

The peaceful, orderly pattern of vibration that is supposed to bring about good health, happiness, hope, love and peace etc. is overthrown, giving rise to sickness, poverty of spirit, sadness, tears etc. That is why we are trying to make like minds to be aware of the fact that PEACE OF MIND is the ROCK, one or more of our great teachers of old and new talked about and are still talking about. It can not be bought with money. It is an attribute (of the mind) that is polished from within the individual. It is a quality of the mind that makes him to be satisfied. This satisfaction arises from the fact that he has known that he is so close to his creator. He loves himself. He knows himself. He has realised himself or discovered himself to such a point that nobody else knows him better. In him, he has realised the inner rock. In him, is unveiled the authority. The authority to construct and shy away from destruction. At that time and this point he realises that those who are known to have natural happiness, joy and good health are those who have or are working consciously towards acquiring the PEACE SENSE and PEACE IN THE MIND. The foundation has to be found and laid properly within.

The ultimate knowledge of the creator is not in the books. Books are deposits of knowledge and experience but the knowledge of the creator transcends book storage. It exists in man's ability to develop himself towards knowing, accepting and serving the creator-GOD. The books lead you to the dawn of knowledge. A step further taken to practise some of the good attributes of the books takes you into PEACE CONSCIOUSNESS.

If you come to the point of knowing your relationship with other units of creation, your major principle will be not to hurt any part of NATURE unnecessarily. You will start feeling that there needs to be PEACE in the minds of everybody because you cannot afford to be a lone ranger having this beautiful state of mind. If everybody has it, the world will be transformed. At this point of mature thinking, the trigger of the gun of ULTIMATE KNOWLEDGE has been fixed into your bare hands. The next thing is to pull it and the bullets that will come out of it will transform you and the world into bliss. Peace of mind is the beginning of wisdom and any man or woman who consciously and knowingly desires it, desires to know the ultimate architect of the whole of our essence. At this point your mind becomes open to positive psychical messages that are far reaching in usefulness to you, your environment and society generally.

This means that, first you have to be conscious of PEACE. Mere cannot be peace on earth if we do not learn to be satisfied with the beauties and bounties on every part of it. To do this, you must get close to NATURE, just the way you see it.

The plants and lower animals have more of the secrets of nature than man. That is why most of man's creations are either copies of NATURE or slight modification of the natural creations of the creator, realised from within, by different men of light at different times. These men used their minds to think and create, not necessarily for their own good and peace but the good and peace and health of man. All that we are saying can be easily achieved by what is generally referred to as CREATIVE IMAGINATION. What we are saying here is that when you start imagining PEACE, LOVE, GOOD HEALTH and HAPPINESS to others and their minds, these good attributes will become part of your mind. You don't want to hurt others except you know that the end of it is good. You don't want evil to befall your neighbours. You feel like protecting them at all times, counsel them and actually want to direct them through the narrow way so that they will not fall prey to evils. This is the PEACE CONSCIOUSNESS, that is, being talked about. This consciousness gradually leads to the acquisition of PEACE IN ONE'S MIND; the rock of ages. At this point you become a leader in your society. You are ready to carry both yourself and others up the ladder of evolution into absolute PEACE

CONSCIOUSNESS. As you progress on this evolutionary ladder, you become purer in mind and more perfect in nature handling. You are now able to eliminate pain, diseases or any other kind of ailment that easily affect man without having to knock always at the medical doors. You are now free of such emotions as hatred, anger, anxiety and all feelings of despair, sorrow and evil thoughts that readily disturb the wholesomeness of your essence and bring about discomfort. It is then that you become or gradually become TRULY HEALTHY and SOUNDMINDED.

LIFE IS LIKE A RAILROAD. THE VAST MAJORITY OF PEOPLE ARE PASSENGER COACHES AND FREIGHT CARS. THEY PERFORM A USEFUL SERVICE BUT THEY CANNOT MAKE THEMSELVES MOVE AND HAVE TO BE PUSHED OR PULLED BY SOMEONE ELSE. ONLY A FEW ARE LIKE THE LOCOMOTIVE THAT MOVES NOT ONLY ITSELF BUT COUNTLESS OTHERS. WITHOUT THEM (MEN OF LIGHT) WE WOULD HAVE NO PROGRESS. HUMANITY WILL STAGNATE AND EVENTUALLY DRIFT INTO SAVAGERY.

John Dickson

CHAPTER TWO

THE EFFICACY OF THE LIGHT

THE MEN OF LIGHT

In history we have come to hear of great men and women who have always worked with the light of God. They healed the sick, opened the eyes of the blind, invented the airplane, discovered the laws of gravity and above all, taught men a possible pathway back into reunion with the light of creation. These men walked on the path of truth and made so much use of the light in effecting positive changes in the destiny of man physically and spiritually. We should not forget then, that when the light shone from the hearts of these men, their lives were never the same again or what was expected by men. The light changed their general outlook at life and the so-called worldly things. So many of them started searching for a better life for all.

It is also known in history that towards these times of deeper yearning for the truth and the light of God, the knowledge of the creator is already abound. That is why the number of those who are now conscious of the light within them and working publicly and silently for the overall good of man has so much increased all over the world.

You see, we want to describe how some of these men of great history discovered the light within them and the accompanying changes that made them to use same to do all the works they did and are still doing. You can be like them, or even more, or have you not heard this before? So many of these men were not just ordinarily wondering about nature and creation. They were quietly asking questions about the existence of nature and their relationship with her. They look at the plants, multifarious with different leaves and flowers. The rivers and the seas, the lakes and the oceans, the mountains and the valleys. The searching man sails along a fresh water river and falls in love with the vegetation and life underneath. "This is beautiful," he concludes.

He looks at the sun and the moon and the twinkling stars. He wonders about the day and the night, the rain and the sunshine, the animals like the male peacock, the beautiful manes of the lion, the feathers of the cockerel, the rainbow etc. He then begins to fall in LOVE with nature, just the way they are. This love now takes him to also wonder about the ESSENCE that has put all these natural edifices in place; the designer and constructor of NATURE. There must be an energy or a supernatural force or something, somewhere that is in control and that is God Almighty.

At this point in time the shield that has been covering the light of the FATHER from you is beginning to fall out. The consciousness of the presence of the creator in you will be on the increase. Ha directs you to a part of a book and the light of God is mentioned. Somebody came close to you and started talking about this LOVE that illuminates CREATION. "This light is in you" is what is always said. So, where in you?

It you listen inwardly, closing your eyes and shutting your oars from external sounds, you will hear your heart beat without using the stethoscope. The sounds you hear emanating from your inside will convince you the more about the numerous activities within. At this stage, the voice of the creator takes over the direction. He tells you, "Look, if I am not here with you, this your heart will not boat. If you can make yourself to believe that I am here, then, you cannot look any further." The day you can settle down in a quiet place or one corner of your room or on your bed and quietly listen to the workings of your heart and body, you would have started on the highway towards 'cooing and knowing the dawn of freedom. You will be surprised that you can stay under this condition for a very long time if you can concentrate.

In this state, your mind becomes free from external distortions. The worries, sicknesses, pains etc. will gradually vanish, if you practise this constantly, over a period of time. It must start from somewhere.

If you go a step further and use your mind to focus any form of natural light that has ever appealed to you on your light, and the inside of your body as if the light is emanating from your heart (centre) and spreading into all the organs, tissues and cells, you will feel a spiritual elevation which could culminate in a deep sleep or a state of consciousness where nothing in the world actually matters any more. This is the feeling called freedom. At this point, you are gradually trying to use the light of the FATHER within you in activating the cells, tissues and organs of your body, for, even the minutest cell of the body is controlled by the same light of God.

This chapter can only be better comprehended and appreciated if you can cast a temporary shadow over all agents that divide men from each other Nationalism, tribalism, cultural differences, religious differences, colour etc. ONE'S mind must be free from these traits to be able to acknowledge the fact that, several men of truth and light have always appeared on this earth from time to time, administering and teaching the people of their various times, how to follow what we call-the way of the light - That subtle light (as they always described it) which illuminates the being from within, and becomes brighter as you realize and make use of it in directing your own affairs and the affairs of humanity, in one form or the other, towards a better expression, positively on the evolutionary ladder.

The lives of the men changed from then on. There are some characteristics that herald the oncoming of the light of peace consciousness and these include:

- The consciousness of the subjective light of the creator in one.
- The moral elevation of one.
- The intellectual illumination allows one to discern accurately (Ability to be submissive and persevere).
- The sense of immortality becomes amplified.
- There is the loss of the fear of death. (Boldness).
- There is the loss of the sense of sin.
- The urge to better the lot of humanity and mankind through the teaching of his discovered way of life (Transparency) becomes amplified.

- There is the added charm and charisma to the personality of the person.

It is better for us to know that it cannot be supposed that, the fact that a man has acquired this consciousness of the peacefulness of the creation does not make him omniscient or infallible.

A summary of the lives of some of these great men is attempted below. The order of arrangement is by no means the order of their importance to human beings and creation. This compilation is not also intended to spite any exact dates that have been compiled or are yet to be compiled by any other school of thought. All that is intended in this treatise is to alert us that men have always been experiencing the illumination of their souls and this has enabled them to bring and shed more light on some of the mysteries surrounding human existence.

In their own words, some of these adepts describe what they saw and how they felt when they passed and got the spiritual lift from SELF CONSCIOUSNESS at which stage you are prone to always protecting your own, into PEACE CONSCIOUSNESS when you try to protect the world, the universe and nature generally. You see, the simple truth is that there has always lived on this earth, appearing at calculated intervals, for thousands of years, among ordinary men, the first faint beginning of a superior race. A race of higher intelligence and propagators of the laws that could enable man to live in peace with his fellow man and to love him knowing that they are just the same. This race has been walking the earth and breathing the air with us but at the same time walking another earth and breathing another air of which we know little or nothing about, but which is, all the same, our spiritual life as its absence would mean our spiritual death. This race has now been collectively born of us and from us and in the nearest future, it will occupy and possess the earth. A gallery of men and women who possess the absolute sense of joyful living.

Humanity has been going on and on almost in despair, hoping that sometime, somewhere, he will find rest and peace and fullness of life in the undefined future, when in fact, all these and more are here row, if we could only reach out our hand and pluck them.

We want to relate to you the experience of a woman in her own words, who was lifted from all her ailments after experiencing the light of God. Her nationality, tribe and religion are not important to us in this collection.

A. J. S.

I was born on the 24 of January 1871, in a country village. I am the seventh of a family of nine and the youngest of six sisters. My family had the musical sense. The girls had fine voices. At about three or four years old, I could sing a song through if it was sung to me. As a result I had the belief that I could be a great singer. I was always very frail. Much of the time, I did not come out to play with other children but liked better to listen to this spiritual music which fascinated me from within. In the end, this dream was dissipated by the tragic death of my father and by an accident that happened to me. My family and friends constantly held the thought of my becoming a public singer before me, and I was sent to a musical school in Boston. It appeared as if my voice had all the quality in spite of my frail physique though some results of the accident appeared to stand on my way. Yet I will not give up.

I was married early and afterwards worked at my music harder than ever and my husband felt that it would probably kill me if I were persuaded to give up. However I broke down entirely as a result of overwork. Everything possible was done for me but to no avail. I was in constant pains and I faded constantly and steadily. I took various melodies to make me sleep but they only brought in more delirium and excitement. I was finally sent to a sanatorium, took to my bed in a darkened room and refused to see any of my friends. For a time, my life was in despair and hopelessness and I only planned to take my life if I can have the opportunity.

At last, a time came when I had given up and felt there is nothing more for me to look forward to than death. One day, while in this state, I was lying quietly on my bed when a great calmness overwhelmed me. I fell asleep only to wake up a few hours later in the night to find myself in a flood of light. I was alarmed. Then I seem to hear the words, "PEACE, BE STILL" over and over again. I cannot say it was a voice but I heard the words plainly and distinctly and just as I heard, I put my head under the pillow to shut off the light and the sound but there they were, so distinct as ever. I lay for what seemed to me a long time. Gradually, darkness crawled into the room again and the sound went off. I was alarmed and immediately sat up in bed. I didn't call the nurse or the doctor because I knew I wouldn't have enough words to make them understand. I did not of course, understand immediately but I knew it meant something.

After that night at the sanatorium, my recovery was steady without the aid of the physicians and medicines in any way. The calmness always came to me often and it was always followed by the light.

After I had left the sanatorium, I still experienced the light and when it came to me while I was in bed with my husband, I asked him whether he saw it but he said he didn't. This is something I really did not try to cultivate but providence brought me into it. I only know that formerly I was a wreck, disillusioned bitch but today, well and strong both physically and mentally. I now love the quiet of home life and a few friends. This calmness has come with the urge to heal others, teach others and direct others towards realisation of the light because I believe that if they consciously search their insides keenly, the flashes of the light of God will appear and become steady within after sometime. When my friends have asked me to tell them of my experiences, I always declined except in one or two occasions. It is all so real to me and I fear that to others it would seem so foolish and sound like a fairy tale. But someday, these things will be explained and I hope that t nay be soon. It is an experience that I lack words to express for poverty of language. To me, it is beyond intellectual expression. It is seeing inwardly and hearing inwardly and the word harmony would perhaps express part of what I was seeing.

My supreme desire was to be of help to humanity, but when I had realised this light come to me, I have been so filled with the desire to reveal what I saw to mankind so that if they try to cultivate this light within them and listen to this melodious sounds coming out of their inside, they may see the light so that they can use it to set themselves free from all bondages but it seems as though I were not doing anything at all.

***

You see, this is the source of all knowledge "the knowledge of the light and sound of God." This leads you to freedom and in as much as all knowledge are derived from the knowledge of God, we may know God better than we know ourselves. This knowledge, if well developed, leads to the LOVE of God and man which is the soul's reunion with HIM – the return of the prodigal son. The reunion of the soul with the light of the creator is like a drop of water realising that it is a part of a mighty ocean and this is the second birth which bears man's immortality and freedom. The woman whose experience was relayed entered into this high level of internal consciousness after so much turmoil and suffering. Must you go through these sufferings before you yearn and look for the light of the creation within you?

JACOB BEHMEN (1575-1624) relates his contact with the light as follows:

The gates were opened to me, that in one quarter of an hour, I saw and knew more than if I had been many years together at a university, at which I exceedingly admired and there upon, I turned my praise to God, for, I saw and knew the being of all beings, the descent and origin of the world and all creatures and creation as a whole through the divine wisdom that was bestowed on me by the light. I am not a master of literature nor of art such as belongs to this world but a foolish and simple-minded man. I have never desired to learn any sciences but from early childhood I strove after the salvation of my mind and my soul and the thought of how I can inherit the kingdom. So I made up my mind to overcome the inherited evil in me, to break it and to enter wholly into the LOVE of GOD in the Christ. I stood by my earnest resolutions and fought a battle with myself with the aid of the mighty hand. At a time I came to notice a wonderful light within me. The light arose within my soul such that when I close my eyes I see the flashes and if I close my ears or I am in a quiet place, I notice the sound within. It is a light entirely foreign to my unruly nature. I notice that it couldn't have been as a result of my good works for, I hadn't much but maybe it came because of my yearning for the love of God.

In this light, I recognised the true nature of God and man and the relationship existing between them, a thing which here to for, I had never understood and for which I would never have sought.

But the decision I took at a point in time is to strive after the salvation of my soul which led me into realising this light.

You will find out that in most of the cases cited, there is this change from the consciousness of the self to absolute peace consciousness which makes them to treat the UNIVERSE and its contents as one whole essence, mating from the mighty source within.

PAUL, in his own words, says, "As I journeyed to Damascus with the authority and commission of the Chief Priests, at midday, O King, I was on the way, a light from heaven, above the brightness of the SUN, shining around me and they that are around me journeying with me. And when we were all fallen to the ground on the earth, I heard a voice saying unto me in Hebrew language – Saul, Saul – why persecutest thou me? And I said, who art thou LORD? And the voice said, I am Jesus whom thou persecutest. But arise and stand upon thy feet; for in this end have appeareth unto thee, to appoint thee a minister and a witness both of the things wherein thou hast seen of me and of the things where in I will appear unto thee; delivering thee from the people and from the Gentiles, unto whom I send thee, to open their eyes, that they may turn from Darkness unto Light and from evil into peace and from Satan unto GOD."

After this time, we are aware of the transformations that took place. The metamorphosis from SAUL to PAUL was packaged in his consequential high moral elevation and intellectual illumination which were so distinct in all his dealings and teachings. In a flash, all his past deeds were wiped away and he became a defender of the light that turned the people of his time and even now, from darkness into light.

The superiority of a scholar over an ignorant man is as obvious as the brightness of the full moon in dark nights.

Prophet Mohammed

PROPHET MOHAMMED's experience of the light happened in the fortieth year of his age. It was narrated as follows:

As Mohammed, in the silent watches of the night, lay rapped in his mantle, he heard a voice calling upon him. Uncovering his head, a flood of light broke upon him of such intolerable splendour, that he swooned. On regaining his senses, he beheld an Angel in a human form, which, approaching from a distance, displayed a silken cloth, covered with written characters. "READ," said the Angel. "I know not how to read," replied Mohammed. "READ," repeated the Angel, "IN THE NAME OF THE LORD WHO HAS CREATED ALL THINGS, WHO CREATED MAN FROM A CLOT OF BLOOD. READ IN THE NAME OF THE LORD, THE MOST HIGH, WHO TAUGHT MAN THE USE OF THE PEN, WHO SHEDS ON HIS SOUL THE RAY OF KNOWLEDGE AND TEACHES HIM WHAT BEFORE HE KNOWS NOT."

Upon this Mohammed instantly felt his understanding illumined with celestial light and read what was written on the cloth, which contained the decree of God as afterwards promulgated in the KORAN. When he has finished the perusal, the heavenly messenger announced "OH MOHAMMED, of a brevity, thou art the PROPHET OF GOD. And I am His Angel."

This is another narration of one of the many occurrences that brought the light of God so close to the people. When a man has yearned for so long for an explanation to the mysteries of life, the saviour comes and takes over to transform him into PEACE consciousness and eventually acquire PEACE OF MIND. At the time when a man yearns for a better fulfillment of his life and creation, most of his questions become bordered on the problems of humanity. Why are human beings unhealthy? Why do they die? So, what is death anyway? Why is there so inch oppression in this my world? Why is there so much inequality?

The questing man will keep on wondering in this state of mind searching but after sometime of this search for the deeper meanings of the mysteries of creation, he surely gets the anointment of knowledge. His soul becomes Illuminated by the rays of the light of knowledge and he becomes enlightened within. If you spend some time in this state of mind, you will stop asking too many questions because you begin to see an order within the seemingly disordered environment.

You become relaxed in your mind because you now know the role of time as the major unfolder of the order of the seeming disordered state of your being. Your questions start having ready-made answers from the higher consciousness that has overwhelmed you and the light of your soul within, waking up your real self from slumber. You wake up to belong to a superior spiritual order. At that time you don't see anything wrong with what human beings do, good or bad. You play with them and dine with them and encourage them through life until their different times of realisation come. When you are under the spell of peace consciousness, forgiveness becomes your watchword, for, the ignorant knows not the intricacies of what they do.

Listen! The hanging gardens of Babylon was one of the seven wonders of the ancient world. Maybe, the idea of cultivating exotic flowers on rooftops and pots hanging on walls has just been conceived and practised, and most people whose power of imagination could not take them up to that level, looked at the practice as a mystery. But nowadays there are millions of such hanging gardens all over the world with more exotic and more mind rejuvenating plants and flowers.

This is analogous to this issue of consciousness that is being discussed here, which is the consciousness of the light of creation and the truth.

The light carried by some extraordinary men and women in the past, is the same as the one being carried now (as it was in the beginning, is now, and ever shall be world without end). The degree of illumination of the inner self (the you in you) determines the various works that has to be done by such a man or woman. To so many men now existing, these great men of old possessed SUPERIOR POWERS, forgetting totally today that even in our midst there are millions of them who have acquired the same light knowingly or unknowingly, many of whom are not necessarily using it to wake up the dead or heal the sick openly or consciously, but are creating some of the things that make others comfortable and at least make others to fuel some content with living. To these group of men (men of light) the light is no more a mystery or something to wonder about. They feel it. They see it with or without casting their minds to it. They hear its sound if they shut themselves from external distractions and noises.

Everybody has the light but in so many, it is simply shielded by the ignorance of it. You will only know of it when the time for you to know comes and somebody tells you about it or you read about it in a book or, in some cases, in time of abject distress and hopelessness. It emanates from within to comfort and reassure you of HIS DIVINE and everlasting presence.

EDWARD CARPENTER

He was born in Brighton in 1844, and he said the following after his illumination or we can say, when he acquired the absolute peace sense:

That day – the day of deliverance – shall come to you, in what place you know not. It shall come but you know not the time. Maybe in the PULPIT while you are preaching the sermon, behold! Suddenly the ties and bands are stripped off and you will become conscious of the oneness of creation. In the cradle and the swathing clothes shall drop off. In the prison, the light shall come, and the chains which are stronger than iron, the fetters stronger than steel, shall dissolve – you shall go free forever.

In the sickroom, amidst life long suffering and tears and hopelessness and weariness, there shall be a sound of wings and you shall think that the end is near (Oh loved one, arise, come gently with me) be not too eager if not happiness will make you shed much tears of joy.

In the field with the plough and the chain harrow; by the side of your horse in the stall. In your canoe while sailing gently on the bright waters of a fresh river or lake. When watching a beautiful sunset or sunrise you become engulfed in the ecstasy emanating from the beauty of what you see.

In the brothel, amidst indecency and idleness. In the midst of fashionable life making and receiving calls; in your dressing room or drawing room, who knows? It shall, duly, at the appointed time, come and the truth will be yours forever, always present to set you free.

Can you see these words of another one of such men and women who were here, then and now, to settle down and teach men how to lay the foundation of knowledge by themselves. This is what we know as divine direction, which is divinely administered for divine changes and evolution.

No human being is capable of stopping it. Whatever anybody does is in synchrony with this divine direction. In the evolutionary ladder of an individual, there are marked experiences. These experiences have been carefully and perfectly designed for you. Your height on the ladder is a measure of how experienced you are in the art of living. They could be good and they could be bad. They could be positive or negative. They all have stamps on the ladder articulately put in place by the same divine hand to ensure the proper evolution of mankind towards the realisation of light and acquisition of the absolute COSMIC sense, that is, that sense of living which a human being acquires at a time in his or her life which makes him to treat every unit of creation as one.

Isaiah 45:3-8 said in the books under inspiration, "I will go before thee and make the crooked places straight. I will break in pieces the gates of brass and cut asunder the bars of iron. And I will give thee the treasures of darkness and show you the hidden riches of secret places that thou mayest know that I am the Lord. I who call thee by thy name and surnamed thee, I am the Lord and there is none else. There is no other God beside me. I have done everything for you: directed, scolded and praised thee, though YOU DO NOT KNOW ME. I am the Lord and there is none else. I have always guided and have always been your chief guard, though you do not know me. That they may know from the rising of the SUN and from the west, that there is no other beside me. I am the LORD.

I FORM LIGHTAND CREATE DARKNESS
I MAKE PEACE AND CREATE EVIL.

I THE LORD, DO ALL THESE THINGS.

There are many parallel verses of this kind in the other HOLY
BOOKS. A second look at these verses above brings one to the
realms of knowing the truth. The truth about the indivisibility of
GOD. You see? Electrical energy is one whether or not it has
positive and negative charges. It is these two charges that make it
electrical energy. Magnetic energy is the same whether or not there
is a north or a south pole. Light and darkness make one day. The
whole thing now depends on how knowledgeable we are to utilize
them to do work.

Now that you are aware that in his hands are the keys open the doors
to the many mansions within you, you surrender yourself to HIM
and He will definitely take control. To a lot of people living today,
the creator is mystery. They look at HIM as an unknowable entity,
so far away in the high heavens. At the same time, they have so
much hope, that someday, sometime somewhere they will come to
know. Something keeps on telling them that one day, the cloak of
ignorance will drop off and the mystery shall be unravelled, the
unknowable shall become a part of their everyday life. At this point
the truth has emerged in you. The light of creation has shone
through and has awakened the soul from slumber. This light now
polishes and reactivates the soul and gradually it will radiate
outwardly. Those who have eyes and are foolish will attack it
because of its suddenness and brightness. Others will absorb it and
start applying it to their everyday life. They will use this knowledge
of the presence of the light to polish themselves and in the long run,

join the chain of men and women past and present who have attained this platform of consciousness to help others along.

We have been talking about how human beings like you find I at one time or the other got illuminated by the supreme light of creation and consequently there was these changes in them which made other humans to wonder because those with this absolute sense use the same to heal, comfort, sympathise with, judge, counsel, direct, teach, create and love others. These same people of light have always reminded us that this light (the truth) is within and can be reached by anybody who asks for it from the FATHER. You have to humble yourself like a child to enter paradise. Relax into HIS HANDS every time. You have to surrender yourself totally to him like the child surrenders to the mother. It is only at this juncture that you experience FREEDOM. Stress will vanish, worries will come and disappear because your mind has no more room for them. Anxiety dies gradually from your mind. The fear of the unknown crawls away. You start losing the sense of sin, because at that time, whatever you do is the creator's doing through you. Your relaxed mind starts radiating from your face. Peace settles down as the foundation of your mind. You start having a feeling that you live forever with your Father and the fear of death wears away from your mind. Your sense of appreciating beauty becomes aroused in you. You start looking at and admiring nature more keenly and you pamper her like a baby. The slogan, "Don't hurt nature so that nature will not hurt you" becomes your watchword. You start to learn how to talk to your father in silence. You gradually become a perfect creation of God... You become born again. You begin to beg and pray for the wellbeing of humanity. Your eyes begin to open to see the perfect design of creation which you are a small part of (a microcosm of the macrocosm). You now become so sure of what you are doing and you start to teach and talk about your experiences to others so that if they follow your teachings somehow, someday, somewhere, they will experience the same freedom.

For it is only when this is done that you can rightly feel relaxed, because as you are now aware only if the others are happy can you be truly happy. Thus you must sustain your efforts at making others peaceful for you to remain in perpetual peacefulness.

CHAPTER THREE

THE WILL TO LIVE

Life can only become sweet if one knows to a reasonable extent, what it is all about. You don't have to wait until you are seriously sick before you imagine what is happening in sick homes. Take a trip to the hospital on sight-seeing and see human beings imprisoned by different sicknesses, in small rooms or in crowded halls gasping for breath. At that point, nobody will tell you to thank your God for even making you poor but healthy.

If you are sick, it means the vehicle that is meant to carry you through this round of existence is faulty. It means that there is a malfunctioning of one of the parts of your body (your car) and it has to be put right. That part must be repaired so that the vehicle (the body) can take you to all your desired destinations.

But the hospital or herbal homes or the spiritual churches or mosques which serve as the repair homes or centres of today are supposed to be consulted as last resorts. In most cases today, they are the first places to be consulted and this is as a result of the veil of ignorance of the power within covering our eyes, which must be shed off. The will to live is that power of the mind that makes you to always want to express life positively and used to psyche the body into good and long life.

We believe that if the will to live is made so strong and well directed, we might in the long run, never actually go to the extent of being imprisoned in hospital rooms with concoctions in attendance. You have to psyche your body into good health. The fact is that, you are here for a purpose and this must be accomplished with a good healthy body taken from the elements of the earth.

These must be returned to the earth at the so-called transition. If the body is sick and the WILL TO LIVE already developed within the mind is given proportionate energy this can be directed to the part of the body which is affected to effect repairs and restore health and wholesomeness. Do not underrate the powers of the mind. The same type of energy that moves towards the sexual parts when a man thinks of a woman seriously can be moved by the mind to infected parts of the body for repair purposes. The fact remains that, one day you will have the need to take positive steps to stay healthy always. If you have not been to the hospitals or slept on their beds before, then, you should start praying that nothing apart from planned sympathy trips or visitations should take you there. For a start into making your WILL TO LIVE strong you have to become very considerate (at least) towards other units of nature so that they can be considerate towards you. You have to think once or twice or thrice before hurting any part of nature. You have to spare NATURE just as she spares you.

You can even go to the extent of sparing the mosquito biting you at times because it has to eat and it has no other farm. There was the story of a man who stopped raising a hand to strike any mosquito perched on his body and this same man stopped having malaria fever which was his major ailment. The fact is that it is your so-called intelligence that makes you the king of the animals but that does not mean that you can eliminate them from nature at your will. You have to pamper nature. Other units of creation have the right to live too just like you but if you must kill them for your food, be considerate enough to let some of them also feed on some part of you too or are you trying to preserve everything for the maggots of the grave? The only thing is that, you, as the king should be able to direct and command them not to transmit anything dangerous into you. The law is that of give and take.

You have to humble yourself into the safe hands of your FATHER. Why are you so proud? Who are you before Him? Humility. Yes, humility is the key into this kingdom of healthiness; that height you climb to in LIFE when you can muster a very powerful and conscious will within your mind to continue to live a good healthy life. If you can handover yourself into his hands every time, He will start carrying you like a baby. At this point you will start feeling the FREEDOM from all the agents that have been pulling you down. There will come a time when the burden would have been lifted from your head, as if in a flash. This freedom, if persistently felt and meditated upon gets transferred from the mind to the body – the beginning of a good healthy living.

You will start to listen to the workings of your body. Some people who have no prior knowledge of biology will acquire books so as to get a good knowledge of their body. You will start counting your heartbeat when observing your silent periods. If it is fast, you slow it down consciously and vise versa.

Your sense of appreciating beauty gets aroused and sharper, that is, you see beauty in almost all things. You become gradually attracted strongly to Nature, its design and her architect. You get strongly assured of the magnanimity of the creator's capabilities and now that you have handed over yourself to Him, you feel that liberation. Happiness then overwhelms you from within. It shines outwards to others who come around you. You now come back to your self and critically examine your mind. You ask questions like –

- Who am I?
- What is my relationship with this world?
- Why are my here?
- Who brought me to this world?
- What type of life have I lived so far?
- So far, what is my most beautiful deed?
- What is my greatest mistake?
- What is my talent?
- What is my greatest strength?
- What is my greatest weakness?
- What is my strongest hope, secret desire and dream?
- What is my greatest fear?
- Am I afraid of anyone? Why?
- Do I hate anyone? If so, why?
- Who do I love most?

- Do I love myself?
- Do I always tell the truth?
- Do I truly want to serve others?
- Do I forgive others and wish them well?
- Am I really as I appear to others?
- What is the truth? Do I know that the truth is an exposition of light to one's consciousness?
- Am I truly the person I want to be?
- Am I really doing the best I can with my life?
- Am I always sick? What could be the cause?
- Am I ready to live a creative life and if so what is my line of creativity? Do I make proper use of my time, energy, talents, mental powers and money?
- If I have failed before, why did I?
- Who has been the greatest influence in my life?
- What would I like most to remove from my memory?

You see, my friend, you have to clear up things in your mind and become honest with yourself and your immediate environment, so that, if need be, you can start to chart a new course for your life directed, this time, by the truth you have discovered within. This light will inevitably shine out of you as a result of an authentic clearance mechanism which you have fashioned out and established for yourself using your mind.

Most of the so-called negative things that happen to us are opportunities given to us to effect changes in our lives. The first major change that is expected of you is for you to tune back the dial of your psychical radio to the frequency where the voice of FATHER-LOVE is predominant. Try and remove all what you consider as evil from your life. Don't wish your fellow man evil. Don't blame anybody for any negative thing that happens to you, instead, anchor it on the fact that the will of the father must be done to shape you to His specification. You take every evil that happens to you as just one of the many experiences that you must acquire in this present life time of yours. You only remind Him (that is, your Father) of the bitterness you had to swallow because of the occurrence.

Eventually, it will get to a time when you will start feeling free amongst human beings. This is so because you don't see them as potential enemies any longer, instead, you look at them as co-climbers on the ladder of evolution towards a better understanding of the life we find ourselves. You did not make yourself. You cannot remember whether or not you consulted your father to make love to your mother so that you can be born. So why do you think that the system that placed you here has no absolute plan for you? Do you give birth to children without trying as much as you can to direct, guide and make good plans for their future?

You have to wake up. You have to look at this your FATHER more objectively. Look and focus your mind on all the wonderful things he has done in your life from the time you became conscious of yourself till date. You will find out that He is always there; guiding every experience (negative or positive). The negative ones are meant to drive you closer and closer to HIM while the positive experiences are meant to encourage you on through the seemingly rough but exciting roads of life. The closer you get to HIM, the lesser the negative experiences become. So, you have to take a decision to be a healthy being in this your life time after all, you are not aware of another. You are the owner of your body. You can always put good engine oil and grease in the right places and fuel in the appropriate places so that you can have an energy packed body ready to explore the beauties and bounties of the beautiful earth where you find yourself The question I need to ask myself now, is that, must my body be subjected to long needles and syringes and almost perpetually administered with big throat breaking tablets before I live a good healthy life?

If you earnestly want to reduce or avoid the doctors' needles, you have to know yourself and your relationship with your FATHER. Are you His child or His goat? Ask questions and after a consistent and well directed seeking. He will give you an answer that will change everything in your life. An answer that will make you to have the assurance that there is an almighty guide around you. You feel an impenetrable armour of light inside, around and over you. There and then, you settle down with a sense of the presence of the spirit of a loving father every time. Anybody, no matter the religious inclination, who starts having that feeling today is already in the Light of God and the same shall set him or her free from all illusions.

A voice, that voice will become constant within you – I am. I am that I am. I always guide you and protect you, though, you do not know me. I form the light and create darkness. I make peace and create evil. I, the Lord do all these things. If you believe this fervently and meditate on this truth as revealed, for some time, a very strong feeling of His closeness will arise within you and your worries will disappear. All the pains and aches will vanish gradually. All sicknesses arising from stress will disappear because He has revealed to you one of the greatest secrets of creation or don't you understand? This is the main secret which the greatest teachers of all times have tried to reveal to men so that the" can live a better life on earth. So, why is it that you don't always want to take a bold step into living a good life, at least, free from sicknesses and sorrows? Can't you hear HIM always saying within you: "There is no other God beside me. When the time is just ripe for you to know me, I use a designed means to bring you back to Me. After so much exhibition of ignorance, I offer you knowledge in a platter of gold and from then on, you live like a king in MY WORLD."

The fact is that, the driver or owner of a motor car who does not understand minor details of the operations of his vehicle ends up, more often, in the mechanics workshop. The man who does not listen occasionally to the workings of his body ends up in the DOCTOR'S WORKSHOP more often. You have to understand your body to a reasonable extent.

You cannot just forget your primary knowledge of biology that tells you that in your body. there is a skeleton holding all the other parts and systems in place. The nervous, the circulatory, the urinary, the digestive and the endocrine systems etc. These systems consist of organs and tissues which serve as processing sites and distribution outfits. If you know where these sites are in the body direct this light you have just realised into them to effect healing and repairs on even the fundamental building blocks of the body, that is, the cells that make them up. Physician, why not heal thyself first so that your method can become a testimony unto others. You have to make this great discovery of yourself so that you will not be a fake physician. One of the great teachers of old made this statement which is still binding on the road to self-mastery. "The God who made this world and everything in it, He who is Lord of Heaven and earth, does not live in shrines made by the hands of men or in other religious mansions made of marble nor is He served by human hands as though He really needed anything, since He himself gives to all mortals, life and breath and all things so that they would search for Him and perhaps grope for Him and eventually find HIM - though indeed HE is not far from each and everyone of us. For in HIM we live and move and have our being. After all, we are also His offsprings."

You can see that you don't have to wait until you are seriously pushed to the walls before you search for the reasons why you are here, who you are and evaluate the journey so far.

You have to discover, through faith and active practice, the doors into the inexhaustible mind within you and also discover the keys to open them up so that you can find a renewed creativity, a flow of powerful ideas, a perception beyond the comprehension of the homo sapien human. You have to discover that this is a universe of law and order and the best way to live in it is to try to realise these laws and order and maintain them.

So, the question is, do you really want to live a healthy, creative and more purposeful life? Then, take a step forward; Discover yourself inwardly. Ask yourself questions. Is this your lifetime just good enough for you to have this final experience of living in paradise on earth? Don't forget that in this same world of today, there are men and women who seldom fall sick, wealthy, always happy with a full dose of peace in their minds. To those group of people, Heaven will not be strange, but there are so many who have not been able to master their stay in the world where they find themselves. This group of people need so much help from those who have seen the light.

HE THAT BELIEVETH IN ME, THE WORKS THAT I DO SHALL DO ALSO AND GREATER WORKS THAN THESE SHALL HE DO.

Christ

CHAPTER FOUR

PSYCHICO-THERAPY

Your mind is the store house of all your past activities, the generator of new thoughts and the receiver of psychical frequencies. All past experiences of an individual are stored in the mind. Some of these past experiences (Good or bad) flash into the present life to teach and put one through. You cannot be a beginner every time, you know? You start from where you stopped every time. The mind is the custodian of all psychical energies. The mind too has the power of concentrating on any of these thoughts. expand on them and if necessary bring them to physical manifestation. There is nothing that has been created by man or ever to be created that did not or will not have its origin from the mind of an individual. This means that the mind is the communication valve between the YOU in you and your body. You and your mind are always together (the spirit) Both the YOU in you and your mind can be separated from the body, temporarily at sleep and permanently at death!

The quality of your mind depends on how far you can fetch from the sea of experiences it has acquired in past times and lives and the extent to which you see and relate with your natural environment. Whatever thought waves the mind generates, it has the power of bringing into reality by directing the necessary and relevant energies to act in the direction required.

The mind also gives you the opportunity of reflecting on your thoughts. Whatever choice of the thoughts you finally bring into fruition depends on the type of experience you need for the record book of your mind.

So you now ask yourself, "how do I make my mind creative so that my immediate environment i.e. my body, and the immediate external environment i.e. the earth and its contents, benefit?" If you have to be creative, then your mind must be impregnated with positivities. You think positive all the time. This is not a way of saying that you should lack the sense of weighing things adequately. I can do it just like others and even better. I can be rich and be satisfied just like others. I can be very healthy just like so many others. And I can have PEACE OF MIND like a few others.

Now take a look at your mind with your mind's eye. Concentrate and evaluate the type of thoughts that always flow across it. Are they progressive thoughts or they are retrogressive to your judgement. Positive thoughts are those that are supposed to bring about a better relationship between you and your environment. You have to resolve to be positive. You have to psychically overhaul your mind and get it oriented towards acts that make you and your environment to live in PEACE. By so doing, you are trying to establish a very good working relationship between your body and the controller within you. Every psychical power you have is in your mind. You only fetch from it to effect changes externally. So can you see that you can kill others or maim others with your mind? At the same time, you can also save others and your immediate environment with your mind.

The latter use of the mind leads you into PEACE consciousness, a state of mind that makes you to see the orderliness in the midst of the seeming entroperical disorderliness. At this time, if your body is afflicted with diseases, you try to use the same powerful mind to clear it first before resorting to the hospital and their drugs. To do this effectively, you must first of all free your mind from all the worries and fears which it is afflicted with. Psychico-Therapy involves, first, clearing your mind and making it capable of picturing things elaborately and then using the same in creatively directing peace, love, good health, joy, wealth etc. into your body and to the minds and bodies of others. At the time when you start doing this, your mind has to be free from negativities at all times and get it concentrated in these positive virtues and they will become yours in practice. Can you see how simple psychic-therapy is? Psychico-therapy also goes further to involve the use of the mind to establish a powerful relationship between your body and the light of your being. Your mind is just a simple link between them. So, the link must be cleared from unnecessary debris so as to be a proper channel of communication.

Psychico-therapy goes further into the use of the mind to look objectively at the mentor of creation. What are your ideas about HIM? Is He great and creative as nature reveals? Is HE perfect as most holy books portray? If He is perfect. then, what is your knowledge of HIM? Are books enough to express His magnanimity? But the books say HE is in me, so, where in me? What is it that controls my heartbeat, which, if not present means "I am dead." Now, if you listen to the beating of your heart and you ask your father – "where are you in me?" – for some time, the voice will come to set you free from all your psychical bondage. "I am the One, I am in you and you are in me. We are one. You are mine and I am yours forever. You cannot be in existence without Me." This will be the new foundation of a new hope in you.

The rock that fails and breaks no more. An endless source of knowledge on whom you can always rely on. This practice described above alone, can take you out of any physical ailment, but still, I want us to go further. I want us to now look briefly at the use of creative imagination in bringing about the ultimate objective of Psychico-Therapy. Physical transfiguration of the body with internal light is the greatest height you can attain with Psychico-Therapy. That means that it gets to a point when your body radiates the light externally from your heart. Transfiguration starts with that of the SOUL, when the light of creation engulfs it thereby taking total control and direction. Next, this same light shines out of you like the star shines from the sky in the night.

Creative imagination is the art of using controlled mental reasoning and picturing to effect changes from the creative energies of the mind and finally influencing our environment positively, hence the word CREATIVE.

Don't forget here that your body is your first physical environment. There is also destructive imagination which always results in jealousy, fear, greed, hunger, wailing, disputes, fights, wars, nucleartests etc. While creative imagination is responsible for moving nature forward in perfection, destructive imagination retards man's evolution. Now, if you creatively and mentally picture the light of the creator just like some of these great men and women saw it, the light will start to occupy and become a permanent part of your mind. Gradually, with series of such imaginations of the same light, your soul will get illuminated. Then, you will notice a change in you. You will notice the truth that the whole of creation is one ocean of light and in order to swim properly in it, you have to work along with the laws that hold it in place. You start to protect the laws instead of trampling on them. You become a proper human being. And when you can imagine this light shining like a glow worm in the dark night, jumping about in your heart in synchrony with your heart beat, you will have an elevation i.e. you will feel very light and free momentarily resulting in a feeling of total freedom from all your pains and worries and who knows, your sicknesses might just vanish with such feeling. This is what we call a spiritual levitation. And if you go further in creative imagination and you picture and focus the light (Like pointing a torchlight) on that part of your body that is plagued by sickness it simply means that you have acquired in yourself what the light did to these great men and women of light in making them whole beings, conscious humans who deserve to be called intermediaries. What the great men of light did was that, after becoming conscious of the light within them, they activated their bodies (even the cells) with it. The extent to which they realised and practiced this revelation is measured by the degree of the inventions

and discoveries they made for the benefit of man, or the quality of
the miracles and wonders displayed by the individual. You see, to
make man to be at least comfortable on earth is a task for all. After
all we are looking forward to paradise or heaven in which system,
you as a being does not suffer sickness, poverty, wars, avarice,
inequality, hunger, tribalism and racism, terrorism and boko
haramism etc.

So why can't you even try to take a step towards achieving one of
the most important qualities of those to be there? And that is trying
to be HEALTHY without the Hospital needles and drugs by
becoming a protector of nature and having peace of mind. Do you
know that there are some people in this same world who are free
from fear, poverty, crying etc. These people are not religionists
because to them, all religions emanate from the same inspiration of
the higher force within. They are not racists and murderers because
they are aware of the RED BLOOD that holds mankind as one.
They rarely fall sick because they have discovered their personal
methods of communication with their father.

They condition their minds against divisions and its agents so that
the world can become one entity, united in all its diversities. At that
time, you reexamine yourself and how related you are to all units of
creation. Finally, you see everything as one, moving, evolving
inevitably towards the same goal. They want people to know God
the way they know HIM so that the benefits in the evolution of
man's soul from crudity to purity with the abundance of the
knowledge of HIM that makes him to be, can be more effectively

appreciated. In the long run, when people stop fighting each other, instead they protect each others' interests, the RACE of the men and women for PARADISE is here. But here on earth, you have to take steps towards acquiring the level of consciousness that brings you to the shores of Heaven on earth before Heaven or paradise in Heaven, you hear?

Man has intelligence and he also has the ability to use his intelligence to see the light and hear the sound of HIS CREATOR (the REAL FATHER) within him. We are not trying to say that he is not anywhere else. In fact, He is in your next door neighbour the way He is in you and in your daughter the same form in you and in your mother just like in you. And in the goat too. The only difference is the experiences of the SOUL of a man in physical bodies that enables him to adapt appropriately towards living in peace on earth. So what we are trying to say is that when you have evolved to the point of looking for HIM within His temple, you realise yourself.

Consequently, you now come to know who you are, your capabilities and your relationship with HIM become blissfully amplified. At that time, you look and reexamine yourself and your relationship with other units of nature. You come to see everything as one moving, and evolving inevitably towards the same goal. So, you come to stop discriminating. You start respecting nature as a whole and the FINAL words that come out of your mouth, then and then is "THANK YOU FATHER-LOVE for exposing a little more of your divine knowledge to my understanding." If you practice and play with the light of your father, the same shall set you free from all your sickness (mental and physical) and all plagues of life forever and you will finally be made to discover the UNIVERSE WITHIN YOU.

CHAPTER FIVE

PHYSICO-THERAPY

According to a magazine publication "a sedentary life style poses more than double the health risk of cigarette smoking" reports the Canadian Medical Post. While some 7 million Canadians are likely to experience serious health problems and early death because of cigarette smoking, between 14 million and 17 million people are facing similar health risks as a result of lack of exercises, and this is the way it is everywhere. Lack of time, energy and motivation are mentioned as major factors interfering with regular exercises of the bodies of so many. Sedentary people are also more likely to consume more fats and less fruits and vegetables. "The current goal for optimal heart benefits is to get people exercising their bodies at least every other day for at least 30 minutes at moderate or higher intensities" says the C.M.P.

The human body consists of the systems, the organs, the tissues and the cells. The skeletal system consists of bones arranged as a frame work for the attachment of the muscles. The joints of the skeleton must be lubricated from time to time like those of the motor car. The muscles have to be stretched adequately and greased to enable the body (your car) transport you on earth through this lifetime. It is so unfortunate that many men and women of today have neglected most of the methods adopted systematically by masters of physical adaptation in form of physical exercises, to lubricate all parts of the body for proper functioning.

In this our age of existence, at least 70% of the living human beings have experienced one form of physical education or the other. It is not the intention of this compilation to give a detailed treatment of physical education but to make us to become aware of the fact that the football or table tennis or the volleyball or the lawn tennis or the golf or the hockey or the cricket or other games you stumbled on in school or elsewhere are designed to set your bones and muscles and ultimately, the cells of your body free from stiffness. Psychical games like chess, scrabble, ayo, draught are designed to keep the mind in good shape and focus ready for Psychico-therapy. So you can see that this treatise on Physico-therapy has a direction, that of directing you into developing the habit of stretching the machine called the body - and getting ready for action before allowing it to undergo regular routine work.

If we want to be factual, at this our range of ages at the time when men were good subsistent farmers, 28 - 55 years, we are supposed to handle the hoe or the cutlass at least three times in a week working hard and sweating to be able to feed at least well, in the village. Hard tough men with well-shaped bodies that are used to hard work. Their bodies were attuned to hard exercises in the farms hence they lived longer in spite of the purported unbalanced diets. So what we are saying is that you can create time for yourself to stretch and mould and massage and strain this your body so that it will not disappoint you at odd places.

There was a man I met on the staircase of an eleven-storey skyscraper. The lift had just packed up. Wonderful! You need to see how a human being – as round as a drum – was rotating up the stairs. Every step he takes, he stops to take a full breath and extra gulps of air. And this man was going to the seventh floor. I followed him behind for some time without arousing his suspicion, then I flew past him taking the stairs in threes. When I got to the third flight of stairs above him, I stopped to see how far my friend has come. Surprisingly, I saw the man has stopped climbing and was gazing after me, apparently imagining what it would be like if he was like me. When our eyes met, he waved to me and I waved back and he said, "My man, I like you. Can I be like you?"

This is just an example of what a sedentary life style does to the bodies of human beings. It makes them flabby and shapeless with a lot of fats which eventually block blood vessels obliterating the free flow of blood to and fro the heart. A little hard job or a minor race makes them pant like a dog that has just finished a very hot chase. All that we are trying to say here is not to mock anybody but to make you realise the fact that if you have seventy years to live on earth, let these years be those of good physical activity. Don't let the football you played in those days in school or the proficiency you had with the table tennis bat or the 100 metres dash you used to do or the strong native dance you used to be so good at just die away like that. After all you are not carrying the hoes and the shovels too often now. Let us try and create a new world of human beings who are physically fit and psychically sound, to explore the earth and bring out its hidden secrets.

Now, talking more seriously, if you are the very shy type who cannot expose some parts of the body in public, then find a way of retiring into a private place. You can lock up yourself in a room to practise physico-therapy. Cast your mind on getting fit always and how to achieve this and you will find out that a series of physical exercises will flash into your mind. Before you know it, you are jumping about, hopping around, stretching your hands and legs and twisting your body in all directions which are strange to the normal day to day activities of the body. You get tired. Take several breaths in and out deeply. If you have the opportunity of playing harder games like football, lawn tennis, hockey, cricket and even table tennis, then you are just the best material to perfect physico - therapy. If possible get attached to sports' clubs. Which ever one of the therapies that is, Room physico-therapy or OUTDOOR physico-therapy, you arrive at the same positive effect after some constant well spaced out practices - A blissful, active, healthy, ready for action, energy packed body.

ROOM physico-therapy is the practice of personally adopted physical exercises at the room and personal level. OUTDOOR physico-therapy is the regular exercises of the body carried out outside by partaking in stronger games like lawn tennis, football, squash, hockey, mountain climbing etc. at least once in a week. If both types of physico-therapies are followed by taking part in psychical games, that is, games which stimulate the intellect directly. like chess, scrabble, ayo, drought etc. Your mental balance will be at equilibrium. As a matter of fact, this is when you become one of the human beings that are trying to inherit the earth. Your body shapes up. You can do physical work without tiring out easily. The fattened bodies slim down gradually. If there is any need for you to run or dive at any time, you will not be found wanting. You acquire a sense of physical confidence anywhere you are, as a result of your acquired physical fitness.

If you are on the sick bed, always try to take in deep breaths and stretch your body on the bed from time to time and gradually your body will assume and adapt to the new conditioning pattern. Don't forget psychico-therapy before physico-therapy is a complete package through the highway that leads to the acquisition of peace in one's mind and a healthy physically active body that can appreciate the beauties and bounties of this earth.

Note: A complete package on PHYSICO=THERAPY ON VIDEO is available on request.

CHAPTER SIX

BACK TO NATURE

There is this energy and centralised intelligence which controls and regulates all the detailed activities in the human being, the earth and all its contents, the universe and the whole of creation. This energy or centralised intelligence has put every detail about creation in place and the best way to tap the best out of it is to learn to co-operate and work along with it. When this is done by someone, he experiences riches of a practical nature, good health of a wonderful nature and joys people seldom dreamt possible. You have to go into a personal relationship with this power and work along the principles which are binding up nature herself and the power that flows will continue to benefit the world. If you practise the principles embedded in this treatise, you will come fully back to Nature. You are a part of Nature. You cannot run away from it. If you see the perfect design of Nature, you will not want to hurt any part of it. Every part of it complements the other, working together for the good of each.

Take a look at the leaves of a well grown coconut tree and compare them with those of the orange tree and the plantain tree. You will notice that there must have been so much creativity put in place to bring about the different designs in them. This type of difference is existent in the more than one million species of plants exhibited on earth.

Take a look at the different animals. There are no two human beings who are exactly the same, even the most identical twins have certain characters which are different. This is the extent to which this MASTER Designer can go into details to exhibit his creativity, beauty and magnanimity to those who are sound in the art of living. Those who are not sound in Nature study, trample on the laws that guide her proper expression and functioning. Those who are very ignorant of the laws step on them foolishly and the law does not recognise ignorance. If you put your naked hand into fire, it will burn it. Now that we have known this, how do we use this knowledge to benefit the world of ours so that there won't be avarice and greed, killing one another, abject poverty, serious embezzlements of public funds, ritual killings- all these are different ways of hurting nature and she will not spare you either. Remember then, that, one who is loving will never lack love. One who is peaceful will never be disturbed. One who is in synchrony with nature will never be harmed even in the midst of confusion and disaster.

Nature is not entirely peaceful as far as we know on earth but even the earthquakes, volcanoes, hurricanes, typhoons, droughts and famine are part of the perfect design of the creator. Since we are co-creators in the creative process of changing the world into paradise we have to remould nature which is a major part of our responsibility on earth. The earth quakes and releases magma in volcanoes in its stabilization process but even all these have not taken more lives than man made wars. For nature to be remoulded nearer to the Heart's desire the law that must be obeyed is the law of LOVE. This law is the least obeyed.

Be still and know that you are that which you desire to be, and you will never have to search for it.

Neville

Think truly and thy thoughts shall the world's famine feed; speak truly and each word of thine shall be a fruitful seed; live truly and they life shall be a great and noble creed.

The P.Ms

Look back and look around a little and you will notice that every serious thing that has ever been experienced by man needs a RITUAL. The ritual is the plan set to achieve a set goal. It might be a set of rules that must be obeyed for a force to be mustered. It could be a series of planned actions that must be undertaken at calculated intervals for a specific result to be achieved. It may be a set of incantations, songs, affirmations. The Olympics has its own rituals. All religions have their own rituals. It is these rituals that contain the differences. The problem with rituals is that the practitioners pay so much attention to the differences between them instead of the similarities which are the foundation for the existence of peace. We are virtually and vitally alive to the degree that we can remain on harmonious terms with nature if we can harness our common rituals and this is the ritual of LOVE. It is the SAME everywhere. LOVE is about giving and regiving, accepting and reaccepting. If you give without a commensurate acceptance, the force of LOVE will not flow. The "giving" we are talking about might not mean parting with one's possessions alone but rendering useful selfless service, like cleaning your environment, tendering your flowers, giving them good soil and wetting them, preaching positive tidings, encouraging others through the vagaries of life and trying to lead them through the narrow path into self realisation where you find wisdom and understanding. When one finds wisdom and understanding, his ways become straight. He lives with nature and nature, in him.

Ah, love! Could thou and I with fate conspire

To grasp this sorry scheme of things entire

Would we not shatter it to bits – and then remould it nearer to the heart's desire.

Rubaiyat of Omar Kingdom, Edward Fitzgerald

Water cannot flow through a blocked pipe. Life, force cannot flow properly through a damaged nerve. Thoughts cannot flow properly through a distorted mind. Creative intelligence cannot function through a clouded human consciousness. You have to be tuned to the frequency of creativity with a balanced mind. A balanced mind is the one that has been illuminated by the light of peace consciousness and has therefore being impregnated with LOVE. When you are in balance, you are spontaneous and decisive. Your timing is perfect like God's. You are patient because you can wait on the Lord. You seem to do the right things at the right time, say the right words and work in harmony with everything that goes on around you. To be balanced, you have to be open to the world within you and the world without.

Meditate on nature, your body (inside and outside), creation generally and you will find LOVE. The force that protects you from hurting any part of nature, for a hurt to any part of it destabilizes the creative force within (God in you) making it to want to express itself somewhere else. You come to see life in everything. You do not want to be the one that will sniff off life from the tiniest ant or fly. You spare the mosquito to suck some blood (its food) for its own survival. What a benevolence?

By the time when nature reciprocates and reveals its design to you, you will be flowing with the divine knowledge of the creator. You start getting lifted from this state of self-centeredness (self-consciousness) into the blissful state of PEACE CONSCIOUSNESS.

If you develop to the point of stepping aside from the world to become a spectator of human activities momentarily during your meditation periods, then you have become an adept. You notice that in spite of the thousands of years that man has become conscious of himself as a human being he has bluntly refused to learn. The crimes of the streets of the world community are drawing back its progress into paradise. Ever since money became introduced into the system, it became the root of all the evils perpetrated by man. They kill each other with various weapons. They steal people's belongings and convert them to theirs. They hurt each other without knowing. What a state of abject ignorance?

President J. F. Kennedy on July 10, 1963 made this address at American University of Washington.

"World peace like community peace does not require that each man love his neighbour; it requires only that they live together in mutual tolerance, submitting their disputes to a just settlement.

"We are devoting massive sums of money to weapons that could be better used to combat ignorance, poverty and disease.

"Let's explore what problems that unite us instead of belabouring those problems which divide us.

"Peace needs not be impracticable and war needs not be inevitable.

"The pursuit of peace is not as dramatic as the pursuit of war.

"Let us never negotiate out of fear. But let us never fail to negotiate.

"All this will not be finished in the first one hundred days. Nor will it be finished in the first one thousand days nor in the life of this Administration nor even perhaps in our life time on this planet. But let us begin."

Let me take you a little bit into history. Ever since the end of World War ll and attendant colossal human and material loss, the world has not known any real peace. It was in an attempt to put an end to a re-occurence of another global war, to promote peace and unity among nations and stop human suffering particularly among the under privileged nations of the world that the United Nations was born in 1945. Unfortunately, the end of the World War signaled the beginning of a new kind of war called the Cold War, ostensibly championed by the United States of America (USA) and the Union of Soviet Socialist Republic (USSR).

The Cold War ushered in the arms race between the super powers and their cronies. The resultant effect is that the world witnessed the outbreak of wars in Europe and in the middle East. Weapons of mass destruction which have long been stock-piled but untested in wars soon found ready markets and usages.

Happy is the man that findeth wisdom, and the man that getteth understanding.

For the merchandise of it is better than the merchandise of silver, and the gain thereof than fine gold.

She is more precious than rubies: and all the things thou canst desire are not to be compared unto her.

Length of days is in her right hand; and in her left hand riches and honour.

Her ways are ways of pleasantness, and all her paths are peace.

She is a tree of life to them that lay hold upon her: and happy is every one that retaineth her.

Proverbs

If therefore ye are intent upon wisdom, a lamp will not be wanting and a shepherd will not fail and a fountain will not not dry up.

The P.Ms

Notable of such wars were British/Argentine war in the 80s, the invasion of Afghanistan by USSR, the Yom-Kippur war between Israel and the Arab nations in the 60s, the Iraq/Iran war in the 80s, the Vietnam war (USA and Vietnam), the Gulf war (the invasion of Iraq by the Allied Forces led by U.S.A. in the 90s). The list is almost endless.

Africa did not escape the grips of the Cold War either, though not known to be capable of producing nuclear weapons and other weapons of mass destruction, many African nations became puns in the hands of the super powers who fanned the embers of war in many African states particularly in the 60s and early 70s. The powers that be not only seized the opportunity of these wars to sell their weapons to various factions, but also propagate their ideologies. Notables are the Congo war in the early 60s and the Biafran war in Nigeria in the late 60s.. Other Nations that had witnessed civil strives in Africa are South Africa with the obnoxious policy Apartheid, civil wars in Liberia, Somalia and the Sudan. Ethnic clashes in Burundi (Hutus against Tutsis).

In Nigeria (Modakeke against Ife, Itsekiri against Urhobo, the Ijaws against Itsekiris, religious riots in Kano and Kaduna, Katafs against Zangos). South south terrorism and Boko haramism.

However, in spite of the gory pictures painted above, mankind have since forged ahead. Leaders of the world realised the dangers posed to mankind by continuing inventions, productions and storage of mean weapons of great human destruction.

Therefore, an era was ushered in which ended the Cold War and therefore the crass arms race amongst the super powers. The end of the cold war brought its own benefits and dangers to peace in the world. It promoted a new spirit of Nationalism and self expression amongst people who were hitherto ruled by Iron hands and therefore could not express their nationalistic feelings for fear of being suppressed and further oppressed. Examples that readily come to mind are the collapse of the Berlin wall and eventual unification of East and West Germany as a nation.

Others are the break-up of U.S.S.R. into various countries which hitherto had been forced into the union, the peaceful break up of Czechoslovakia into two nations, Czechs and Slovaks; the end of Apartheid policy and regime in South Africa and eventual release of Nelson Mandela, the fratricidal disintegrating of Yugoslavia into Croatia, Serb and Albania (Kosovo), ethnic clashes/genocide in Burundi, the independence of Eritrea from Ethiopia.

The wind of change blowing through the world as witnessed today is as a result of the conscious need and yearning of the people of the world and their leaders for peace to reign all over the land in order to prevent poverty, hunger, homelessness and many other social injustices that results from conflicts.

It is the belief of the Peace Merchants that the world is presently witnessing three revolutions which are social/political, economic and psychical in nature.

The social/political revolution will eventually usher in a high level of political order in the world and break up social, political, tribal/ethnic and religious boundaries as we are gradually witnessing in the world today.

The economic revolution, will eventually rid the world of poverty and usher in a world where life is treated as sacred and the necessities of life are within the reaches of people. The third revolution, the Psychical Revolution (mind Rejuvenation) is the unconscious and conscious need of people to search for peace, in the world. They have seen the evil effects of conflicts and they yearn for change into a world of utmost freedom. Freedom from visas and passports with the belief that the whole of the Essence belongs to the same creative force. They do so by radically becoming PEACE CONSCIOUS. They talk and preach peace using many Global occurrences. They fervently believe that a day shall come when man would have experienced so much evil emanating from conflicts and consequently faced with the bliss of peace.

The two revolutions mentioned earlier, no doubt will radically change the conditions of, and greatly uplift human lives, but the Psychical Revolution will attempt to do more.

The three revolutions operating together will inadvertently create a new order of things.

If one takes a look at the manner by which certain Global issues are being resolved nowadays, one would agree that there are certain people who are undergoing the revolution of the essence of life in them (SOUL) without being conscious of this fact. Before now, people were so self-centered to the point that their minds are almost oblivious of things that make life amiable with other components of our existence. Hence, it is now pertinent for people (especially leaders) to evolve a new system of things, devoid of greed, avarice and hatred and usher in the next stage of the ladder, which is, living with others in PEACE, LOVE and HARMONY.

At the time when the MIND searches for PEACE, it has reached a point of understanding the laws and order of NATURE, and the need to work along within the frame work of these laws and order so as not to infringe against any. Therefore the evolution of the human soul is very dynamic positively and cannot stop at personal consciousness (which is the father of SELF-CENTREDNESS) into what the PEACE MERCHANTS refer to as PEACE CONSCIOUSNESS. In order to accomplish that transformation, a revolution must be and must have been at work silently in the minds of some people from time immemorial. This has made it possible for a few of human beings to have acquired the absolute peace sense. Great men like Socrates, Moses, Isaiah, Mohammed, Jesus, Buddha, Mahatma Gandhi, Osonobrughwe, Oduduwa and so many other present-day sages who are either directly using the knowledge of the light in effecting changes in the lives of men or creatively inventing things scientifically, technologically, economically, politically etc. to make human life comfortable on earth. When one takes a look at the lives of these men and women who acquired the peace sense, one finds out that when they were alive, they had no earthly religion nor stuck to their tribes but at the same time all the tenets and ethics of religion absolutely dominated their lives.

A peace conscious human being is the one whose mind has developed to the point of undergoing this revolution and transformation into PEACE CONSCIOUSNESS. Therefore one finds out that most people today are undergoing this great metamorphosis. They are worried about the nature of things as they stand today, and want to effect peaceful changes by appealing to the human minds in order that most of mankind be carried into this realm of consciousness thereby fulfilling the dreams, hopes and aspirations of leaders and teachers of the past.

You see this is why we are the PEACE MERCHANTS. Our methods are subtle, persuasive but firm and we hope to touch individuals and groups alike with the arrow of light illuminating the path of PEACE in our hearts designed by the Architect of this whole living essence called our world. So, you will find out that you are back to nature.

NOTE: The simple use of the names above has nothing to do with their spiritual and exalted positions with mankind.

EPILOGUE/CONCLUSION

Don't blame human beings for anything that happens to you. Blame providence for placing you exactly where you are. Maybe the pressures of birth and death (one or more soul cycles) have made you to be ignorant of the fact that you are the divine director of your providence if you so believe. If you don't know this and start directing your providence it will continue to direct you.

You have to know yourself and your relationship with your creator so that you can use HIM to change the parts of your destiny that are hurting you. The simple process is what we have given to you in this pamphlet.

The dropping of the atomic bomb on Hiroshima and Nagasaki in Japan brought about their withdrawal from the second world war. The Japanese decided to go back to the drawing boards, not to design bigger bombs but to re-evaluate themselves. The implementation of the draft that came out started with the science of self-mastery. They introduced this even in schools. Just before studies in the morning, the students are made to observe about an hour of silence and mind concentration. They stay with themselves even in the midst of the classroom crowd. And the result today; a virile country with human beings who are no longer trouble seekers but men and women filled with the knowledge of remolding nature and its abundance into physical wealth.

So if a country can mobilize her people to collectively go back to the drawing boards to reexamine herself so as to be able to know her weak points and probably use the energies abound to reshape them, why not you an individual who has the same potentialities of a country do the same.

You as an individual cannot be endowed with everything. You have one or two or three talents that you have to discover in yourself. Identify your talents and try your hands on them with vigour, directing every energy in you towards getting the best out of them and you will end up making yourself a hero. You become a hero in your field. Ask every great man and he will give you the same story. Man know thyself. That was what Japan did. They discovered that they don't have the necessary machinery and personnel to win a world war. So, they withdrew from it and decided to direct all their potential energies towards making Japan an economic and industrial power and not a mediocre warlord and they are the better for it.

Don't put a blockade between you and your father. Don't allow religion to take you away from your creator for He is not a religionist. So why can't you try to be like HIM. Most of the intermediaries we talk about as our messiahs today were in the long run misunderstood and they became objects of worship. They came to show human beings the way to see, speak with, be directed by, hear and get used to, the light of the creator which they (Messiahs) already have realised. That is why so many of them will not allow themselves to be worshipped but the ignorant human being seeing signs and wonders displayed by them turn their adoration to them instead of to the ONE who is using them. Some of these men of light (both old and new) get carried away by manly worship and forget to tell their followers, listeners and admirers to know that they themselves are ordinary tools used by the creator to reveal more of His inexhaustible knowledge to man at appointed times and you can be one of them. So my friend, wake up and become the child of God and get mature so that you can call your father a name that befits Him. A name with meaning and activity so that when you call Him by it He will not hesitate a second to change your stresses, strains and emotions and remold your destiny into a blissful one. You can have the mighty father to yourself alone by calling him a good name and so can others have Him to themselves alone when they learn to call Him privately and quietly. At the time when you want the mighty father to change the bad circumstances and experiences of others into bliss, then, you are gradually becoming a messiah.

Man as small as he is, can alter his lot in life by intentionally controlling his mental states, attitudes and state of consciousness. Every prophet or messiah has proclaimed Inspiration Books like this one are not to be read and discarded like ordinary novels. They need some degree of disciplined reading and practice. If the principles work for you, okay, if not, you drop them and look further. One day, somehow you will come across the ones that are just meant for you, to work with you and reshape your life into bliss. What is given to you in this compilation is Divine knowledge in a platter of Gold. Use it only for the progress of man, the Universe and its contents.

APPRECIATION

I want to thank the authors and publishers of any books, journals and any other references from where we got some of our quotations. They should have known that the truth can never be hidden for ever, and they were only brought out for better use by man, whether they were contacted or not. We love you.

the P.Ms

I thank the following men and women for their constructive criticisms and straightening up of the treatise: Mac Nelson Adekolu Adewunmi, Sam Ojame Adedeji Murphy, Ahmed Abiodun Onaneye Bimbo, Lilian Nwabueze, Otung Bassey, Osaghale Strong, Adjose Hundeyin, Cookey Felix, Olukunle Damilola, Yoroh Charles, Olowoyo Bunmi and Adeniyi Olu.

vvww.peacemerchantsinternational.com

ABOUT THE AUTHOR

A 1982 graduate of chemistry from the University of Ibadan, Richard Oyovwevotu Efemuaye is a seasoned educationist and a director with the Lagos State Government.

He found out that if ordinary atoms can show so much love by losing and gaining electrons. humans can do better if they wish each other peace the universe will experience peace.